PoetProblems...

*Table of Problems...*

September 21, 2016

I told you so.


I would rather hear

'If you didn't know

Now you know'

Than to be told

'I told you so.'

Because I could easily

Tell you some shit

That would change your standpoint on life...

Probably wreck your soul.

You may come out alive

Maybe even look fine

But you know nobody is the same

After a bad wreck, on the inside.

September 3, 2016

Provocative


Come get it.

Come get this

> *Provocative*

Biting your hips

Wait..

Just let me handle these love handles

Real quick...

...spread your hips.

Let the anticipation build up slowly

Float into my smoke cloud.

Crack that Hennessy

Let me see if I can ease—

Lets.. lets transfer that stiff in your neck

Down your spjne to the small of your back.

Just do me one favor

Try not to scream too loud

Try not to.. snatch my soul

When im deep.. groping my throat

Labeling yourself on my collar bone

Intertwining our fingers.

Im trying to see if I tease your spot

Will the euphoria of me exploring you linger?

August 1, 2016

Make-Believe.

*"the thing about make believe is that..*

*If you can make yourself believe it, then others will eventually follow suit."*

Its funny..

Because I think I just realized

That the lump in my throat is loneliness—

The degenerating appetite

The tears being strong in my eyes-

They hold themselves up so that I don't need to waste my time

Like I needed you to fill my void.

I used to get so easily annoyed

And now I just avoid you.

...because I know you have a boo

But I don't need my thoughts to be anointed by you.

You...you'd think you've rubbed up on enough

And other things not so much..

But that's a sensitive area to touch.

I always have intentions on being petty

But the wounds that I break open are my own.

And I only do it to spark the attention

That I could never keep from you—

When had the pleasure of keeping you...

You know, when you claimed to be happy.

Because I know that you will save me.

I'll have you in my grip again

And you'll proceed to act like

You've never been awaken at 2:47am

To find me restlessly crippled

That you never only cried at the thought of losing me.

And I'll brainwash myself into thinking that

The table you're sitting at

Is 46minutes from your house

And I'm running around the room

Pretending not to eaves drop

On you telling your friends that—

**That I'm the one.**

For old times sake

I'll just pretend.

I will pretend that

I never hugged anger from your spine

Or kissed comfort onto your lips.

Pretend like you never gave me peace

Because now you pretend like

My pain shouldn't exist.

Now I'm trippin.

So, I'll just pretend.

I will pretend that

We were only ever friends.

I will pretend that

I don't miss your touch

When im watching Netflix

Every now and again.

I will pretend that

I look at you with virgin eyes.

Even if I have to excuse myself

To throw up these lies

And wash it down with Hennessy..

Even if my last breath is loud

You probably wont hear a sound.

Lets see if I'm silent

Will you pretend to hear me.

January 23, 2017

Reasons.


I get upset with people

For reasons that I wont even allow myself to explain to them.

I got reasons for reasons

That would be insane to them.

And I let a lot of shit slide.

I tell a lot of little white lies

That lie dormant until I shut my eyes to sleep.

So, now they wanna meet and greet

Chop and screw through my unconscious mind...

Who would've ever thought that a little white lie

Would have questions that have answers to find?

Im having confessionals while im asleep

Im talking reasons so deep

I cant LET that shit roll off my tongue

So, my true beliefs are never released.

I've learned to face the world with fearless eyes..

Im not saying that's a bad thing.

In return, I strong-body every potential threat

And everything that may seem to be

And im not saying that's a good thing.

Did I mention that I get upset with people

For reasons that I wont allow myself to explain?

I got people that got reasons to avoid my name.

I destroy everything important to me

That includes people.

They think im not home

While im staring through the peephole.

February 7, 2017

SomeDaze.


Some days make me scream

For sundaes

Because everybody knows that ice cream

Makes everything okay.

And some days

I scream for Sunday

So that I can get a little mercy.

My problems are getting proper

They say excuse me and they curtsy...

All I want is some peace.

Guess I never expected a test

Just a testimony

Because I thought I had already seen everything

And God was like

"Watch the show, B"

Go ahead God, show me.

So, He provided myself

With the resources to get to know me

And I don't mean to sound selfish

But this shit is kinda lonely.

Some days

Take me by storm and trample me

Shit flying everywhere

Obstacles coming like a stampede.

Then some days

I bounce back like a trampoline

Hit the ground running like it's the ram in me.

I supplement my dopamine

Im always praying for some mercy

Excuse me please, my granny prays

So, its just the faith in me.

February 6, 2017

Sultry.


I forgot that your eyes shine like

I think I forgot about paying FP and Light..

Skin a little scarred like exit wounds.

My mind took a flight last time

So, I missed you.

I managed to stay awake

I've been counting down the days..

I knew I'd see that ass again soon.

I couldn't let you just skate

This time, so I kissed you.

Such a bold personality—

Subtly intimidating.

You emit tranquil waves.

Im just admitting you humble me

You know I don't like to behave.

No shade, ya baby kinda act like me

Fuck around and end up with matching nikes

Now, you and me have to just do it.

I've been ready all night

Im ready to get to it.

You are my poetry shrine

The place I go to unwind.

You just happen to be fine

From outside to inside

Even down to your time.

April 18, 2017

'Complacent'

-   Showing smug self-satisfaction, accompanied by
    the unawareness of potential or actual dangers or
    deficiencies.

Show me you mean it

I'll show you unimaginable shit.

The type of things

That make you think about bouncing around and shit.

I'm kidding

You not gonna wanna miss a single scene of this.

Complacency

Will be the death of me—

If you're adjacent to me at the end of this.

Baby

Your ignorance is that Omega kinda bliss

I become the Alpha when I release it from your lips.

The type of shit—

Have a homo sapien doing donuts in club Twist.

I'd rather be complacent

Than let paranoia take the hit.

March 26, 2017

King.


I..um..

I love you.

You always know how to say what to do

      And you never apologize for it.

So, I respect that.

Because you're the only man

That does not have to force it.

You demanded to let no one have control of your life

And that's something I can understand

Because your words weigh heavy

And your actions are equal on the other hand.

You're the realest one I know

I never expect anything from you..

Never had to put me in my place

Or gave me a reason to run from you.

You were raised to be a king...

I could never address you as anyone else.

Your knowledge moves mountains, baby

Your aura is stealth.

December 14, 2016

Bare Skin


If you can bare the wind

Just bare with me..we're gonna win.

Comparing now to way back when—

I didn't have so much permanent ink embedded in my skin.

I think it's kinda fine

When I find a dime with bare skin.

I appreciate your nakedness

No lines to hide anything between.

I love that you're so raw

Bare, I mean.

So smooth, a baby's bottom would get jealous

That body is angelic

But that attitude is hellish.

That's 100% chocolate though

So.. its cool. I understand that.

If it's really that good

I think you need to brand it.

February 5, 2017

Fit.


People try so hard to fit in.

I try hard to fit people, though.

It always stabs me, ya know?

This is how rollercoasters go

And I hate em.

Check this out.

We're gonna start off slow

Ima give you this 4in blade to fend off your foes

5 seconds pass, you've already got it at ,y nose,

What's that text about?

Hmm.. he's nobody important.

So, about our day we go.

You say you're fine like I don't know

I keep my intuition on the low

And remain distant.

A couple weeks of odd behavior

Now you're 2 inches deep.

You've paved a path of mistrust within me

Im not really one to envy.

Talking to you is just a chore.

I have a REALLY bad habit

Of spoiling my women

Before they return to their men

3 deep, im only running on adrenaline

So I still gotta have it.

I've heard of women wanting

To want other women to fit in.

But have you tried to unbite an apple that's been bitten?

It's more intense than a feeling.

Its deeper than fronting.

It's handing someone you DON'T trust

A 4 inch blade...

Got 5 inches deep before I could walk away.

I knew better and did that shit anyways.

All in the name of lust.

May 22, 2017

Proud.

-having or feeling a high satisfaction for one's achievements, qualities or possessions.


To be very pleased

Is an overstatement.

And THAT'S an understatement.

We're unimpressed.

We were raised under high standards—

Importance was always a normality.

Sugar-coating shit don't change its composition...

We don't chase our liquor..

Fuck a technicality.

*exhale*

We embrace that thump in the chest

What other way to determine if we're alive?

We've been ensured that no pain, no gain

Since we last cried at the age of 5......

We're in our twenties now, though.

So, the months go fast

But the years go kinda slow.

May 25, 2017

Sensitive.

-quick to detect or respond to slight changes, signals or influences.


Some of us need to be BOLDLY labeled with

"HANDLE WITH CARE".

They feel the slightest part of everything so strongly

While the other half of us

Are on that half dead, half witt

"ima STILL give you life

Because ignorance IS bliss" type of shit.

Which side relly possesses bliss?

If seeing is believing

Then it's not the side that hold their eyes open when they kiss.

hh.. excuse me, miss?

I noticed your aura felt a little dim

Could I just polish your crown a little around the brim?

May 22, 2017

Age.

-the length of time that a 'person' has lived or a 'thing'
has existed.


Age ain't nothin' but a number

Until you're 28 and haven't seen anything.

Your brain caged

Like free-range chickens that lay eggs

With no personal space—

So, they barely grow.

Thoughts still in baby stages...

Your body has been here

But your mind has been M.I.A. through important phases.

What do you really know?

I know tired souls at 23

Just trying to greet the end of 2017.

Rappers talkin' about 'more life'

Like we haven't already had enough...

These cats always want more.

Everybody knows that curiosity

Took all 9 lives at once

And everybody still want to explore……

July 28, 2017

Magic.

-an extraordinary power or influence seemingly from a supernatural source.


The church once said

That Eve was bred from Adam's rib...

I took that to mean

That women possess a little bit of magic.

Actually, I've witnessed that as a matter of fact—

So, I had to approach the stand as a witness.

If her look could kill

Then I've overdosed 147 times

But it's hard to confess what really happened.

S, I plead the 5th-

..of whiskey, that is.

I say blame it on the liq and set her free

But, honestly...

If God made a whole gender from a rib

Then who's to say she can't influence a brain

With only the touch of a fingertip?

December 29, 2016

Merry.


A starving artist

Is stereotyped as a nearly homeless individual

Incoherently banking on talent......

But I maintained a job!

And I hid from the people

That were blindly watching me fall apart

Then had the audacity to question

                        HOW I was 40 pounds

lighter.

I can tell you that the pain in my heart

Was trumping anything my stomach could scream.

In the public eye, I remained serene

Until somebody disturbed me..

They say make a joyful noise unto thee

And if you can't be nice

Then you shouldn't say anything..

                        So, I don't.

They say we can definitely make it if we try

All we need is a will

                              But, I wont.

How did I get here?

In and out of doctors

My car doesn't want to change gears.

I have a new store manager

And she's sexing the stupidest cook there—

The one that's always tryna fight with me.

My job is in between us on the line, b.

I raise my voice sometimes

I don't mean it, I swear..

I just need people to hear!

My heart is young but my soul's been here for years.

I found myself living to learn

Because I'm dying to be understood.

I went from being robbed by property management

To knowing everyone in the hood.

June 1, 2017

5:48


I'm always up at the buttcrack of dawn

Along with the butt end of your thoughts...

They weren't sent for me

But we usually crash.

I can see each and every regret

That's biting you in the ass

And they're biting chunks at a time

So, there's not much left for me to hold.

 That last line was a little bold

Because to you, my views have never been told

And they never will.

I just noticed you got a lot of dopeness to spill..

It flows freely throw the cavities you can't fill

So, you appear fine.

Still shoot shit with the guys

And get high out ya mind—

So, no one knows what lies behind those eyes

Because they still shine...

And that's fine, nena.

I see yourself and see, that's dope..

A little subtle motivation

To remind the kid there's hope.

June 10, 2017

Word.


-a single distinct meaningful element of speech or writing, used to form a sentence and typically shown with a space on either side when written or printed.


Okay, so…

What's the difference between

                              You and a word?

You're both distinct and meaningful;

Both have a space on either side of you—

You're both single.

I said, I noticed no one's occupying

                              Any space on either

side of you.

I'm claustrophobic, too….

You wanna mingle?


                              Hm.

What IS the difference between you and a word?

A word doesn't really have a brain and curves

But it could be a rose by any other name

With a quick weave and a pretty face.

I guess you two are <u>not</u> the same.

I could find many words...

But, to pass up the chance to permanently admire

A rare sight?

I wouldn't find another in this life.

June 20, 2017

Black Women


Black women have

Never been respected.

That's why I love to see a

Black woman

In charge.

I love my women...

You ladies take up space

Within my heart.

You keep our black men out

Of the dark.

Beautiful and smart—

Know that the love will

Never part.

I respect you.

June 8, 2017

12:58


I roll my best leaves at 12:58am—

When I'm trying to debate who tf I think I am.

They claim beauty is a trait

But my panel wont agree…

I've witnessed beauty be stalked by pain

In a predicaments where

beauty was never meant to be.

I sit in loud clouds

Trying to unsee things

And my sun's still drawn in the corner of my page—

Off to the side, I drew a tree

To kinda minimize the shade

And I'm usually in a daze.

So, we're gonna let bygones be bygones

Because when the flesh fades

We're gonna differentiate the riders from the pythons.

June 4, 2017

I swear I'm good with words…


My honest goal in life is to

Make panties drop with my poetry…

My words are contagious

My vibes have high potency.

I speak to a few women with pick-up lines in my eyes—

A couple do reply

So, lets try conversation…

I'm thinking I'm good with words, so just try

But, oh my……

I think my anxiety is calling on the other line…

Could i.. could I call you right back?

I'm embarrassed 'cause the kidd got many words

Then, my verbs make the kidd wack.

It's just a little crazy 'cause

Poetry drips from my tongue

Like the flow I created.

Expressions cum to my head

Like when she's flexing her abs, trying to hold it in
instead.

My goal in life is to make panties drop with my poetry;

I swear I'm good with words....

May 28, 2017

2:53


When I met him

He had the biggest crush on me.

A couple months of 'secret' dinners and lies pass by—

Now he, and she, rest in peace to me.

And me?

I can never rest, b.

She spent days reiterating

That I was daddy.. but she was witty.

Now he's Bobby, that bitch be Whitney.

She spent days convincing me

That I was perfect.. but she was slow--

Because as the days turned to weeks..

I caught on, but she didn't know.

So, I still let her go.

We'd discuss it after I built my courage up from blowing down;

While she was out being a peasant, I pawned her fucking crown.

Oh, now she look dumbfound

Because I thought I was a snoop.

But what time could I allot to come find her ass?

Needless to say she was a fool

Because the Third Eye sent screenshots to the group chat.

I never thanked her for introducing me to that...

She never thanked me for passing him off.

Maybe she should thank herself for that, though

Because I would've bitten her head off

Then wiped my mouth with a red cloth...

May 3, 2017

Shade.

-1) comparative darkness (or obscurity) owing to the interception of the rays of light; 2) an unreal appearance.


With a presence so evanescent

I bet you contain a lot of shade.

I bet you shun off parasitic vibes

And play people like spades.

Not a King or a Queen

Just a Jack of all trades—

Trading Hearts for the Clubs

So many Diamonds down to play.

March 17, 2017

PiscesSeason


I've seen things unfold

Faster than they could be assembled.

I've conversed with people so humbled

Their anger would make the ground tremble.

I'm trying to figure out

Why 'woke' is what everyone wants to be

Meanwhile, I've been 'woke' for awhile now

And I'm ready to catch some z's.

I wished for things

That I thought would be easy to obtain—

So, now I'm careful what I ask for.

I'm still a little skittish

Because I've already asked for a lot more

And I don't know...

Pisces Season got everyone pressed about being awaken

But this is not just a snapchat filter

Posing for the cameras will get you taken.

September 6, 2016

PoetProblems.


Imagine walking through

Every life changing experience T W I C E.

The second go-round being

The death of your soul

From personifying what you lived….

THAT is the gorgeous tyranny

                          Of being a poet.

If I had to choose another way to do it

I'd rather die twice, multiple times

Than to not know the intensity it takes to live.

They say that

Is it the burden of unspoken words

That ultimately tears us apart—

But the dopest spoken word

That I've ever heard

Was recited by torn hearts.

  …I'll just leave that there…

But society has your vision impaired

So, you probably won't see that.

And don't even look my way for love

I probably won't be that.

March 18, 2017

Precision.

-the quality of being precise, exact.


She described something of rich quality.

She ensured that I would feel

Relaxed as if it were lavender

And sleepy like chamomille.

She compared it to caramel

Because I like sticky and sweet—

She didn't leave a mess on my cheeks

Because precision is key.

She pulled back her hoodie

I took a shot of that, neat

By the time it hit the back of my throat

The strength had left her feet.

Women aren't that hard to please

Her aura changed—magenta pink

Her soul looked over at me

As her pride laid her body across my knees.

March 20, 2017

feel.


I used to daydream

About how amazing forever would 'feel'...

Now, I couldn't give a shit.

'love-sick' was my sidekick when I confronted you

I, then, threw my guts up

And spat my heart back at you.

I'm numb now

That's what I strived for, boo.

Never feel a thing—

That's the rule of thumb;

Third finger to the ceiling

10 toes down, mean I'm the 1*.

"all these bitches is my sons"

Know that I don't really want kids...

The other night

A negative bloodline confirmed that

                              I don't really
'want' shit.

She said that.. I don't 'feel' anything.

I'm thinking "how the hell you know that?"

On second thought though, I'm thinking

I don't really wanna know that…….

She was right, though.

I didn't feel as if I should attempt to deny it

I be acting like I'm exempt from cryin'…

But I teared up a bit.

I worked hard to be so numb

I developed a love for it.


December 2, 2016

TheFeels..


I want to say more

I just cant..

Unless I'm writing it down

Or on a rant.

So many spectrums around me

All I see is pink.

Notebooks, pussy, clothes

Even when I blink.

To think.. I actually thought that

Adulting would be easy;

They warn that life gives you lemons

But lemonade requires squeezing.

Btw, chicken does require seasoning;

Actions should have reasoning;

While some of yall out here treasoning

I'm just tryna find a meaning.

Strange doesn't begin to describe

How I know the 'what' and not the 'why'...

But maybe every fucking fire

Is the end result of a lie.

Maybe every single flood

Is the personification of the tears emotions you cry..

Maybe your worst day of every year

Is a foreshadow for the day you die.

Made in the USA
Middletown, DE
22 May 2022

65947443R00029